Contents

Any words appearing in the text in bold, **like this,** are explained in the glossary. You can also look out for them in 'Body language' at the bottom of each page.

Nobody like 'em!

Take a look in the mirror. You will see a very familiar face. But there isn't another face like it in the world. It is **unique**.

There are millions of people in the world. Every single one is different. Identical twins are the most similar people. But even they are not exactly the same.

There are millions of faces in the world. But no two faces are the same. This is partly because of how we choose to look. It is partly because of genes.

unique unlike anything or anyone else

Body Talk

In Your Genes

GENETICS AND REPRODUCTION

EXPRESS
EDITION

Steve Parker

www.raintreepublishers.co.uk
Visit our website to find out more information about **Raintree** books.

To order:
☎ Phone 44 (0) 1865 888113
▤ Send a fax to 44 (0) 1865 314091
▥ Visit the Raintree bookshop at **www.raintreepublishers.co.uk**
to browse our catalogue and order online.

First published in Great Britain by Raintree, Halley Court, Jordan Hill, Oxford, OX2 8EJ, part of Harcourt Education.
Raintree is a registered trademark of Harcourt Education Ltd.

Produced for Raintree Publishers by
  Discovery Books Ltd
Editorial: Kathryn Walker, Melanie Waldron,
  Rosie Gordon, and Megan Cotugno
Design: Philippa Jenkins, Lucy Owen,
  John Walker, and Rob Norridge
Illustrations: Darren Linguard and Jeff Edwards
Picture Research: Mica Brancic and
  Ginny Stroud-Lewis
Production: Chloe Bloom
Originated by Modern Age Repro
Printed and bound in China by South China Printing Company

10 digit ISBN 1 406 20416 1 (hardback)
13 digit ISBN 978 1 4062 0416 2 (hardback)
11 10 09 08 07

10 digit ISBN 1 406 20423 4 (paperback)
13 digit ISBN 978 1 4062 0423 0 (paperback)
11 10 09 08 07

British Library Cataloguing in Publication Data
 Parker, Steve
  In your genes! : genetics and reproduction. - Differentiated ed. (Body talk)
   1.Human genetics - Juvenile literature
 2.Human reproduction
   - Juvenile literature
  I.Title
  599.9'35
A full catalogue record for this book is available from the British Library.

This levelled text is a version of *Freestyle: Body Talk: In Your Genes*

Acknowledgements
The publishers would like to thank the following for permission to reproduce photographs:

Alamy Images **pp.18; 5, 4-5** (Visions of America); Corbis **pp. 6-7, 8; 20** (Luis Enrique Ascui/ Reuters), **pp. 26-27** (Walter Smith), **p. 36** (Bettmann), **p. 42** (Gabe Palmer), **pp. 14-15** (Charles O'Rear); Getty Images **pp. 5, 17, 26** (Photodisc), **p. 31** (Photonica), **pp. 32-33** (Taxi), **p. 41** (Stone), **pp. 42-43** (The Image Bank); Getty Images News **pp. 16-17**; Science Photo Library **p. 22; 5, 23** (TEK Image), **p. 7** (Simon Fraser), **pp. 9, 28, 29** (Steve Gschmeissner), **pp. 10-11, 35** (Eye of Science), **p. 13,** (Corbis/Digital Art), **p. 21** (Dr Paul Andrews, University of Dundee), **p. 25** (Du Cane Medical Imaging LTD), **pp. 37, 38** (Edelmann), **p. 39** (Garry Watson), **p. 40** (Alex Bartel); The Advertising Archives, **p. 24**.

Cover photograph of baby reproduced with permission of Masterfile/Pierre Tremblay.

The author and publisher would like to thank Ann Fullick for her assistance in the preparation of this book.

The paper used to print this book comes from sustainable resources.

Dedicated to the memory of Lucy Owen

The same, but different

People everywhere are alike in many ways. Our bodies are basically the same. We usually have two eyes, one nose, and so on. And we are most like members of our own family.

The reason for our similarities and differences is deep inside us. It is in our **genes**. We need to find out what genes are and how they work. Then we can understand what makes each of us unique.

Find out later ...

...what needs 47 pairs, while you only have 23.

...what a **genetic fingerprint** is.

...why some people have dimples and some do not.

Instructions for life

Imagine you are building a computer. You have all the different parts. But you also need a building plan. This shows you how to put the parts together.

You build the computer. Next you must programme it. This means giving it working instructions. These tell the computer how to do different tasks.

We use instructions to build ➤ a house. The body uses its own set of instructions to build itself. These instructions are called genes.

Building and running

The body has plans and instructions too. They show the body how to grow from a baby to an adult. They also tell it how to work and live.

But a body's instructions are not written on paper. They are inside your body. These instructions are called **genes**.

Different types of genes

Genes affect how you look. They decide your skin colour and your height. They also carry instructions for making inside body parts.

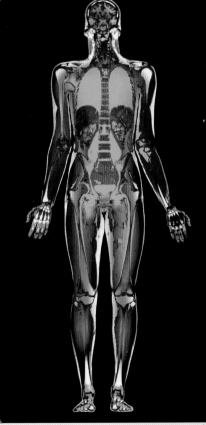

genes instructions for how the body grows, develops, and works

Building blocks

Any big machine is made up of lots of small working parts. The human body has more than 50 trillion! These tiny parts are called **cells**.

Different cells

Your body has many different types of cells. They have different shapes. They also have different jobs to do. For example, long thin cells make up your muscles. Spider-shaped cells make your bones.

Fingerprints

Fingerprints are the swirly ridges on our fingers. The pattern is controlled mostly by genes. No two people have the same fingerprints.

Skin and hair cells "switch on" only the genes that they need. They switch on skin and hair genes.

cells   tiny "building blocks" that make up all body parts

Take what you need

Each cell contains 30,000 different **genes**. These are your body's complete set of instructions.

But a cell does not use all these genes. It only uses the ones it needs. So a muscle cell has the "muscle genes" switched on. They tell the muscle how to do its job. The other genes are switched off.

Where are genes?

We are used to seeing instructions in words and pictures. But the body's instructions are very different. They are in the form of a thread-like substance. This substance is called **DNA**.

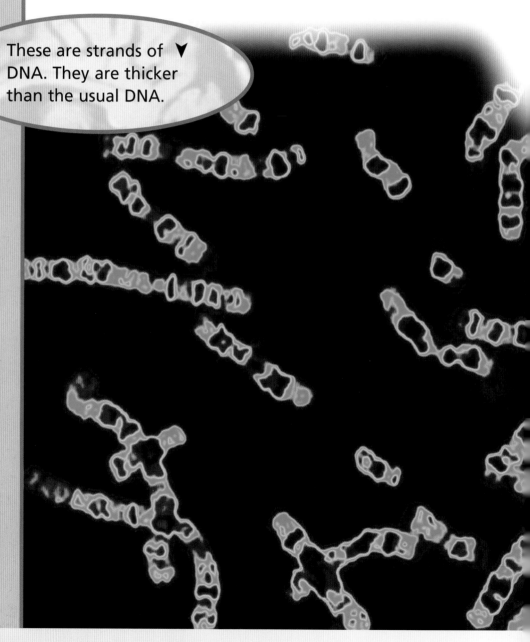

These are strands of ▼ DNA. They are thicker than the usual DNA.

DNA (deoxyribonucleic acid)   substance that contains the body instructions, or genes

In the control centre

The body is made up of trillions of **cells**. Near the middle of each cell there is a rounded blob. This is called the **nucleus**.

Each nucleus contains 46 strands of DNA. These strands carry your body instructions. They tell all parts of the cell what to do.

Size of DNA

✦ DNA is very long. It is also incredibly thin.

✦ Imagine you could join all the DNA in your body. It would stretch from the Earth to the Sun and back more than 100 times!

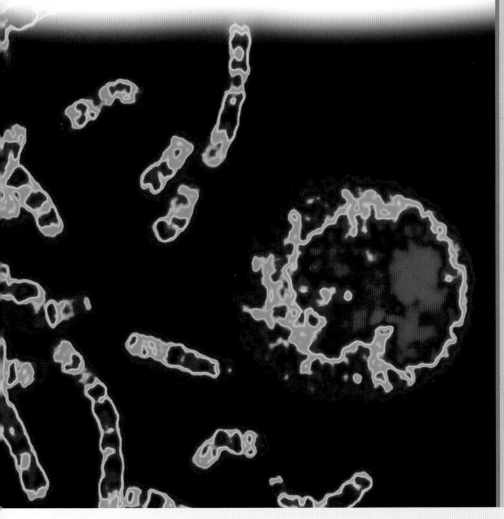

nucleus control centre of a cell

What shape are genes?

Genes are instructions for your body. They are stored inside **DNA**. DNA is a long, thread-like substance. It is shaped like a twisted rope ladder (see picture on page 13). The two long sides of the DNA ladder are the same all along.

But the cross parts, or rungs, are not. There are four different types of rung.

Written in the genes

A gene is one section of a DNA strand. The order of its different rungs spells out an instruction. It tells the **cell** how to make something.

This is how cells know what colour your hair will be. It is how they know what shape your face will be. This type of information is written in your genes.

DNA (deoxyribonucleic acid) substance that contains the body instructions, or genes

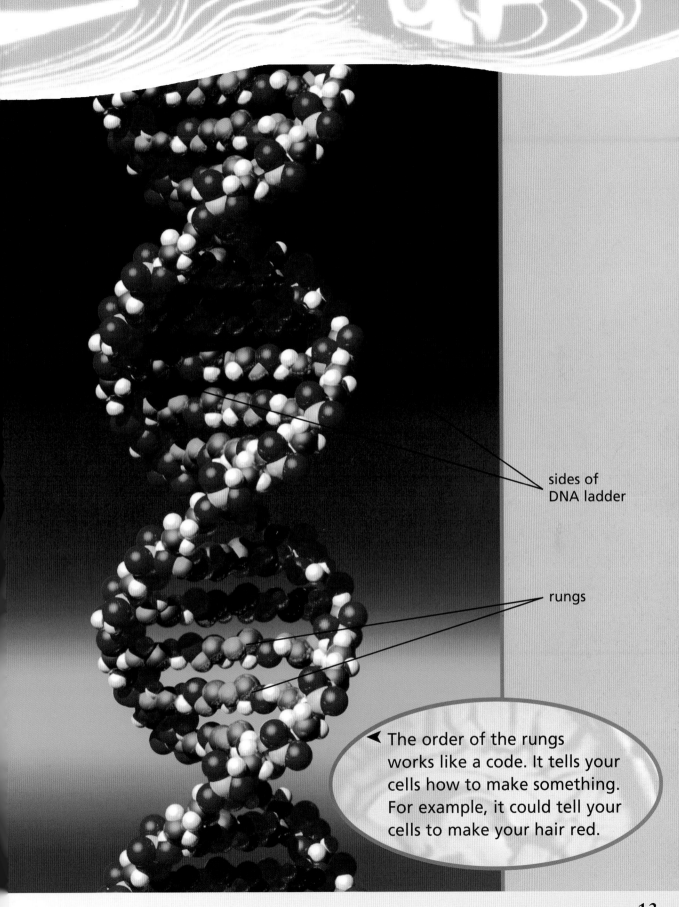

sides of
DNA ladder

rungs

◄ The order of the rungs
works like a code. It tells your
cells how to make something.
For example, it could tell your
cells to make your hair red.

cells tiny "building blocks" that make up all body parts

Working plans

Your body is made up of millions of tiny **cells**. **Genes** are like building instructions for the cells.

Genes are kept in a cell's **nucleus**. The nucleus is in the middle of the cell. It is the cell's control centre. The cell makes copies of the genes. It is like making copies of a computer file.

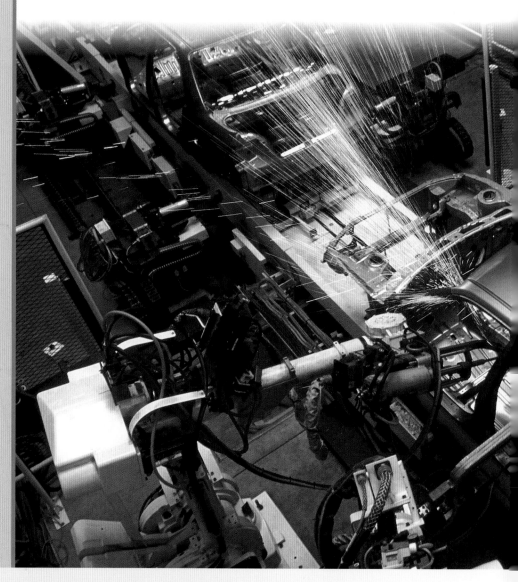

nucleus control centre of a cell

Building work

The copies move out of the nucleus. They give instructions to other parts of the cell. The cell begins to make new building blocks for the body. These building blocks combine to make new body parts. Different body parts are made from different blocks.

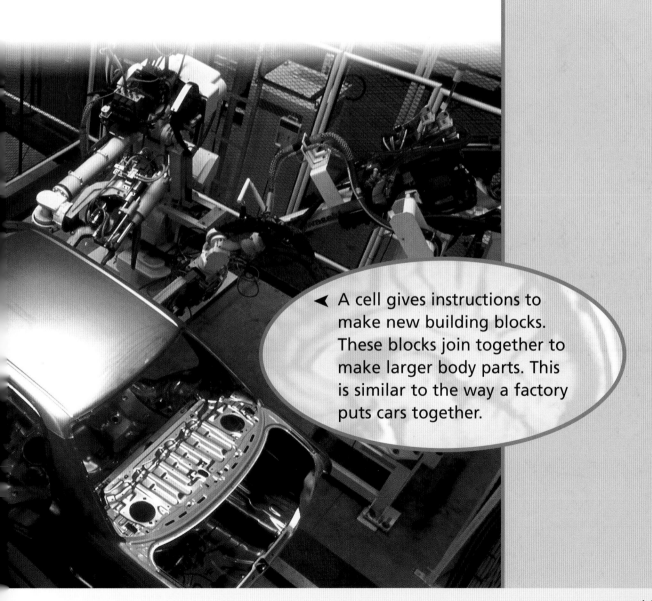

◄ A cell gives instructions to make new building blocks. These blocks join together to make larger body parts. This is similar to the way a factory puts cars together.

Pair of genes

Genes provide instructions to your cells. Most of your body **cells** contain two sets of genes. Therefore a gene is one of a pair.

A gene is one part of a **chromosome**. Chromosomes are long strands of **DNA** (see page 12). There are 23 pairs of chromosomes in each human cell.

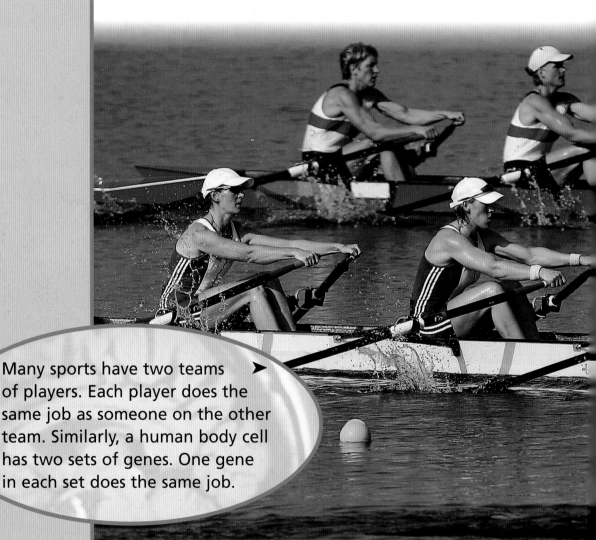

Many sports have two teams of players. Each player does the same job as someone on the other team. Similarly, a human body cell has two sets of genes. One gene in each set does the same job.

chromosome thread of DNA

Two genes for one

Both genes in a pair are often the same. They contain the same information. This is for making the same bit of body. For example, you have one pair of genes for making eye colour.

But in some pairs the genes are slightly different. You might have one gene for blond hair and one gene for dark hair. These differences make you different to everyone else.

More and less

Other animals have pairs of chromosomes like us. So do plants. But most have a different number of pairs.

Fruit fly	4 pairs
Human	23 pairs
Goldfish	47 pairs
Crayfish	100 pairs

DNA (deoxyribonucleic acid) substance that contains the body instructions, or genes

Giving orders

Do you have long, dangly earlobes? Whether you do or not depends on your **genes** (body instructions).

You have two genes giving instructions for every part of you. But the two don't always give the same instructions. Some genes have different versions. You get one version from each of your parents.

Dimple test

Genes control whether or not you get dimples in your cheeks. The "dimple" gene is stronger than the "no dimple" one. So just one dimple gene will give you dimples.

dominant when one version of a gene is stronger than another. The dominant gene's instructions are followed.

Trial of strength

Both earlobe genes might be dangly versions. This will give you dangly earlobes. Or both genes might be small versions. Then you will have small earlobes. But what if you have one of each gene?

The small earlobe gene is **dominant** (stronger). The dangly earlobe gene is **recessive** (weaker). The stronger gene wins. You will have small earlobes.

GENE FOR	DOMINANT GENE (stronger version)	RECESSIVE GENE (weaker version)
Hair colour	Darker hair	Lighter hair
Hair loss (men)	Early hair loss	Late hair loss
Eyelash length	Longer eyelashes	Shorter eyelashes

Which gene is boss?

Many genes act in the same way as earlobe genes. In the table on the left, you can see which genes are stronger.

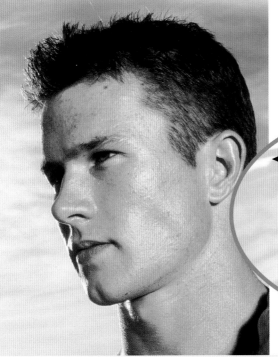

◄ The older man has dangly earlobes. He must have two genes for dangly earlobes. The younger man has small earlobes. He may have just one gene for small earlobes.

recessive when one version of a gene is weaker than another. The recessive gene's instructions are not always followed.

New cells for old

Five million tiny parts of you die every second. These parts are **cells**. But about five million new cells are born every second.

The body is always replacing old cells with new ones. It uses **stem cells** to do this. These are cells that make new cells. They do it by dividing in half. Both halves then grow to full size.

Different jobs

Each new cell can stay as a stem cell. This means it will divide again. Or it can become a different type of cell. It could become a muscle cell, for example. Then it will no longer divide.

Stem cells

Stem cells can become almost any kind of cell. Medical scientists (below) are studying how to make them become particular types of cells. This could help sick people.

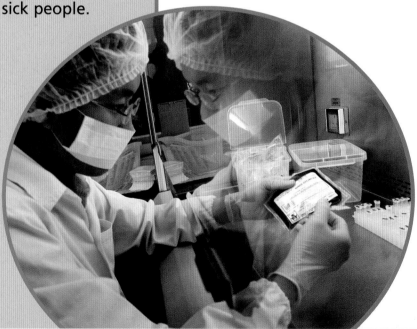

cells tiny "building blocks" that make up all body parts

▲ This stem cell is dividing. The two new cells will grow to full size.

stem cells   cells that can make many different kinds of cells

Copy, copy, copy

Each body **cell** needs its own set of instructions. Strands of **DNA** contain these instructions. So when a cell divides, it needs to copy its DNA.

DNA unzipped

DNA is shaped like a twisted ladder. To copy itself, a strand of DNA "unzips". It does this by breaking apart at the rungs (as shown here). This produces two half-ladders.

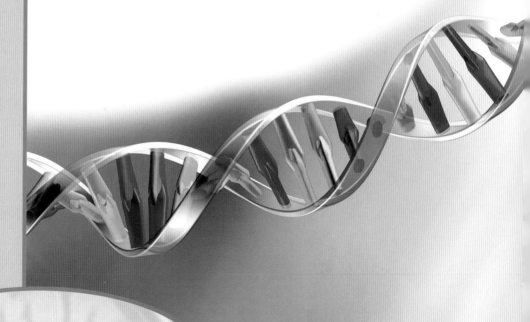

To copy itself, DNA splits down ➤ the middle. Each half then builds up a new half. This will be an exact copy of the old one.

Body language   **DNA (deoxyribonucleic acid)** substance that contains the body instructions, or genes

Two the same

Each half-ladder then builds a new half. The result is two new ladders. These ladders are strands of DNA.

DNA rungs unzipping

DNA fingerprints

Scientists can find out how a person's DNA is built. The pattern of the DNA rungs (see page 13) is called a **genetic fingerprint**. Each person has a different genetic fingerprint.

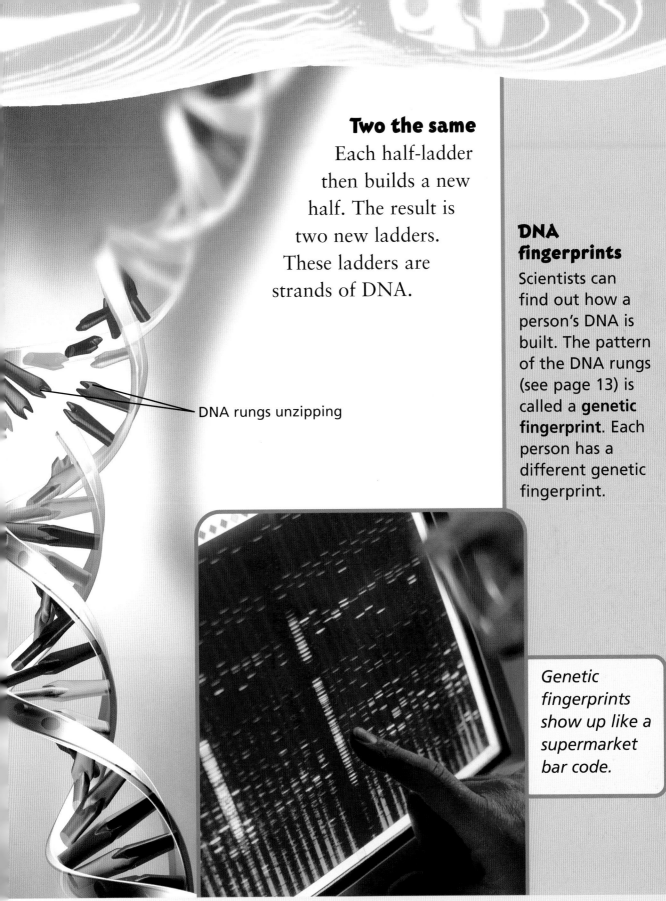

Genetic fingerprints show up like a supermarket bar code.

genetic fingerprint code on a strand of DNA. This code is different for each person.

Not exact copies

If you copy out lots of words, you will probably make a mistake somewhere. You might miss a word. You might write the same sentence twice.

It is the same with **DNA** copying. DNA is copied when a cell divides (see pages 22–23). But sometimes a mistake happens.

Ultraviolet (UV) light comes ▼ from the Sun. It can damage DNA. This may cause skin growths.

Mistakes and effects

Several kinds of copying mistakes can happen in DNA. These mistakes are known as **mutations**.

Mutations can have different effects. Some cause trouble. They can cause a growth, or **tumour**. The growth can make you sick.

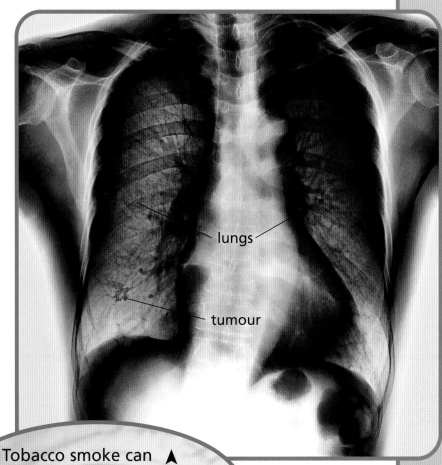

lungs

tumour

Tobacco smoke can cause changes in DNA. The changes may cause growths in the lungs.

tumour abnormal lump or growth

Members of the same family often look alike. This may be the colour of their skin and hair. It may be their ear shape. We say there is a family likeness.

Many of these features are passed from parents to children. Then they pass to grandchildren. This is because of **genes**. Genes give instructions to the body.

Missing out

Sometimes a grandparent has a body feature that the parent doesn't have. But then the grandchild gets it. This can happen with red hair (below). It happens because of the way genes work.

Inheritance

Each person has a double set of genes. One set comes from the father. The other comes from the mother. This passing on of genes is known as **inheritance**.

◄ Family likeness is strongest between parents and children. This is because their genes are most similar.

---

inheritance   when something gets passed from parent to child because of genes

New beginning

Every human body begins as a single tiny **cell**. This cell is made when two other cells join together. One of these is an **egg cell** from the mother. The other is a **sperm cell** from the father.

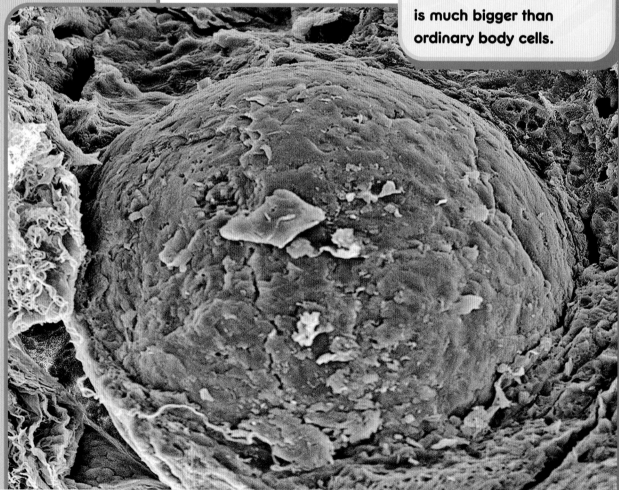

Two ones make two

Most cells have two sets of body instructions, or **genes**. But egg and sperm cells have only one set.

The egg and sperm join. Their single sets of genes come together. So the new cell has the usual two sets of genes.

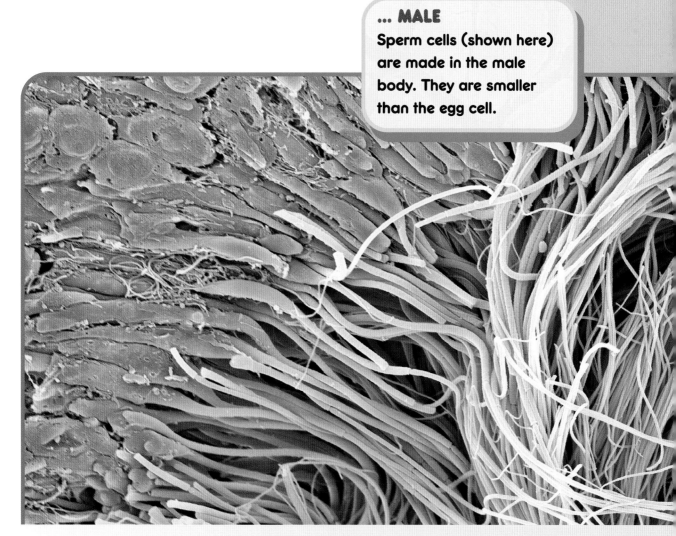

... MALE

Sperm cells (shown here) are made in the male body. They are smaller than the egg cell.

sperm cell   cell made by the male body

Reproductive parts

Male and female bodies have mostly the same parts. But some important parts are different. These are the ones used for **reproduction**. Reproduction means making babies.

Egg release

Egg cells are made in the female. They are formed in two rounded parts. These are called **ovaries** (see below). About every 28 days, one egg cell leaves the ovary.

Female parts

The female reproductive parts (see below) begin to develop at the age of 10–13 years. The time when they start developing is known as **puberty**.

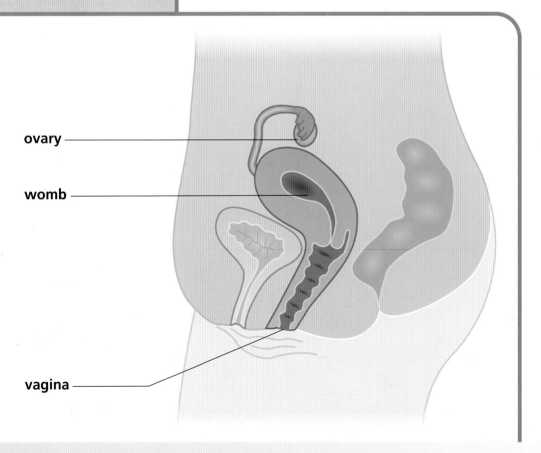

ovary

womb

vagina

puberty   when a human's reproductive parts begin to work

Journey to the womb

This egg then moves along a tube. This tube links the ovary with the **womb**. The womb is where a baby develops.

Four or five days later, the egg reaches the womb. A baby may develop in the womb if the egg has been fertilized. A **fertilized egg** is one that has joined with a sperm.

◄ The reproductive parts of the body do not work during childhood. They start working during puberty.

womb   female body part where a baby develops

Sperm production

Sperm cells are made in the male body. Thousands of them are produced every second.

Ready to leave

To leave the body, sperm has to travel through a tube. Fluid is added to the sperm during this journey. The fluid helps the sperm to swim along.

Male parts

Every day millions of sperm are formed inside the male body. They are made in the two **testes** (see diagram below).

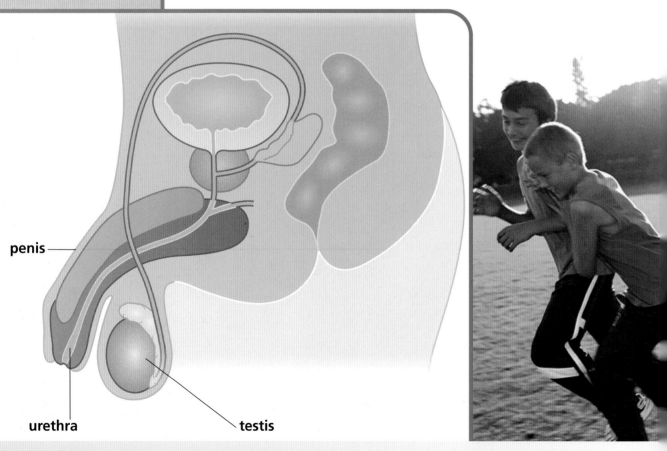

penis

urethra

testis

testis   part below the male body. The two testes make the sperm cells.

The final journey

The sperm and its fluid then pass along another tube. This is the **urethra** (see the diagram on page 32).

The urethra carries the sperm out of the body. A muscular action makes this happen. The action is called **ejaculation**.

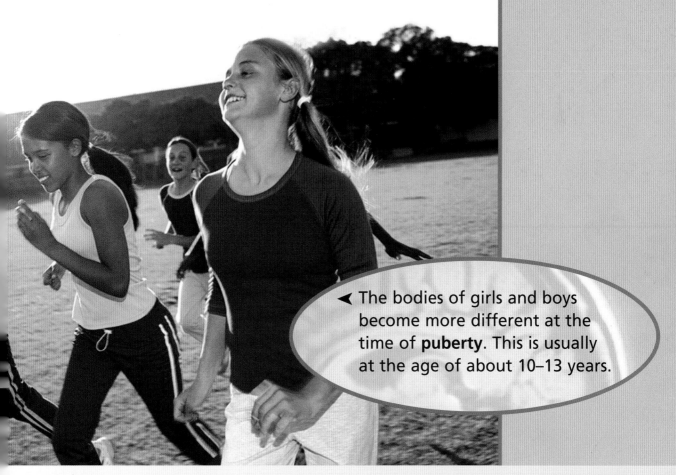

◄ The bodies of girls and boys become more different at the time of **puberty**. This is usually at the age of about 10–13 years.

ejaculation muscle-powered action that pushes sperm out of the male body

Getting together

Sperm cells leave the male body through the part called the penis (see diagram on page 32).

This may happen when the penis is inside a female's vagina. The vagina is a passageway. It leads to the womb or uterus. A womb is where the baby grows.

Genes come together

Sperm cells swim through the womb. Then they swim out along two tubes. The egg cell is in one of these tubes. Some sperm cells reach the egg cell. One pushes against the egg. The two cells join.

Together the two cells form a new double set of body instructions (genes). These will control how the baby develops.

penis   male body part. Sperm is released through the penis.

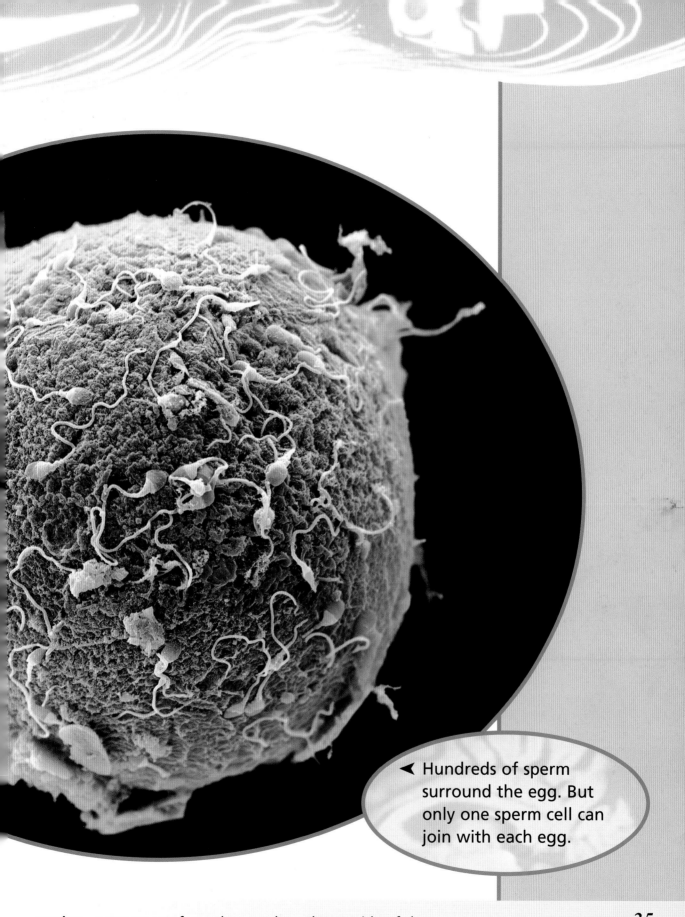

◄ Hundreds of sperm surround the egg. But only one sperm cell can join with each egg.

vagina   passageway from the womb to the outside of the female body

New baby

Every new human begins as one **cell**. After a few days it is a ball of cells (see picture on page 37). It moves into the mother's **womb**. Here it continues to develop into a baby.

Girl or boy?

The baby's cells contain 23 pairs of **chromosomes**. These carry the **genes** (body instructions). One pair of chromosomes decides whether the baby will be a boy or girl. This pair is known by the letters X and Y.

▼ Sometimes more than one egg leaves the **ovary** at the same time. When this happens, more than one baby may be made.

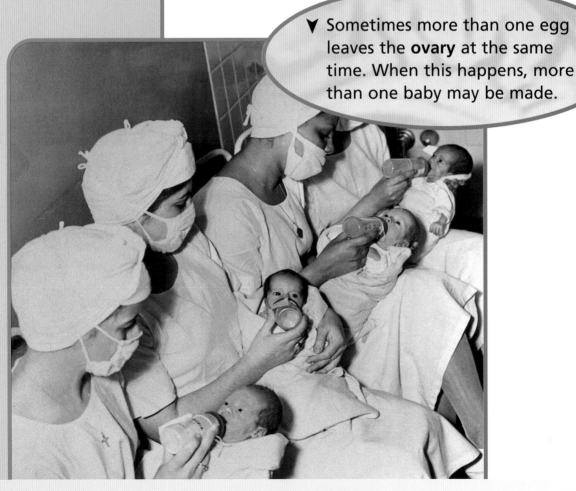

chromosome thread of DNA

X and Y

The mother's **egg cell** always carries an X chromosome. X is for making a girl. The father's **sperm cells** can carry either an X or a Y chromosome. Y makes a boy.

The father's sperm cells decide the sex of the baby. If a sperm carrying the X chromosome joins an egg, it makes a girl. If the sperm carries the Y chromosome, it makes a boy. This is because Y is stronger than X.

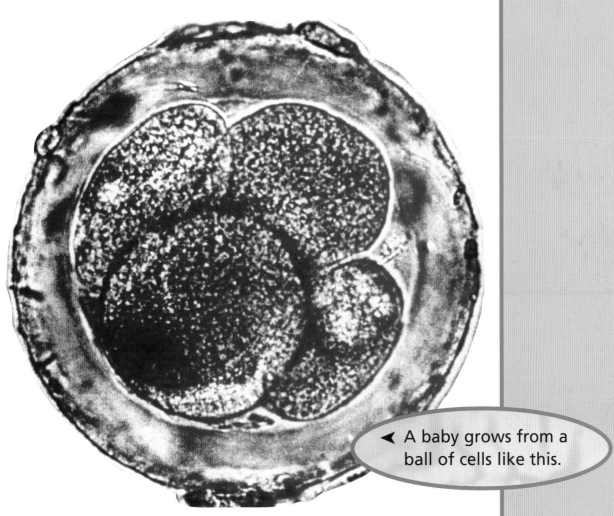

◄ A baby grows from a ball of cells like this.

Life in the womb

As the human body starts to form, the **cells** divide quickly.

For the first eight weeks, the baby is called an **embryo**. At the end of this time its main body parts are formed.

Life support
Inside the **womb**, the baby doesn't eat or breathe. It gets all it needs from its mother.

▼ This developing baby doesn't look like a human yet. This is the embryo stage.

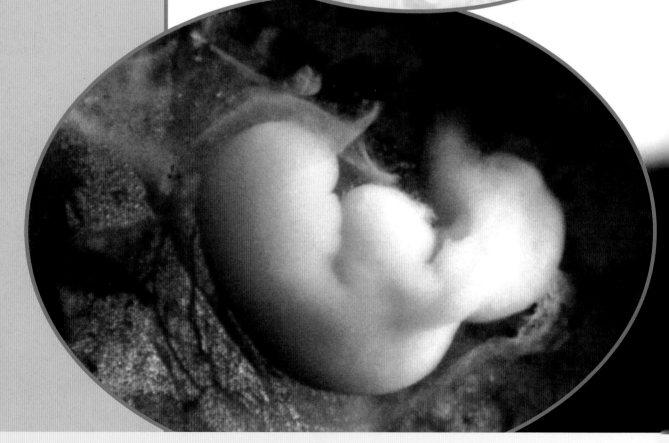

embryo developing baby that is less than eight weeks old

Pregnancy

From eight weeks until birth, the baby is known as a **fetus**. Its body parts become bigger and stronger.

The whole time of growth in the womb is called **pregnancy**. This normally lasts about nine months.

The fetus stage begins after about eight weeks. This is when the baby begins to look like a tiny human being.

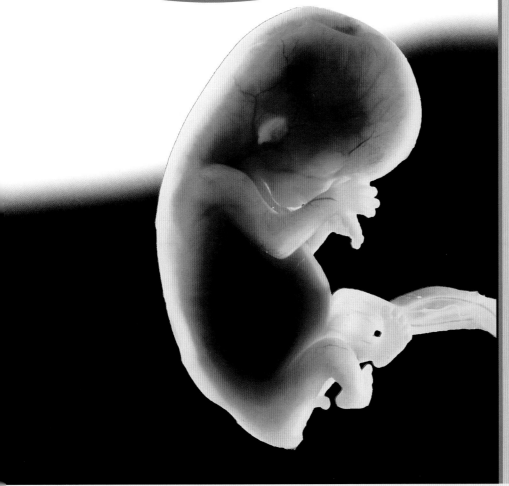

Identical twins

Sometimes a **fertilized egg** (one that has been joined by a **sperm cell**) splits into two. Both halves may develop. They will make identical twins. These babies have exactly the same **genes**. They look very similar.

fetus developing baby in the womb, from eight weeks old until birth

It's your birthday!

After nine months the baby is ready to be born. At birth the baby begins to breathe for itself. It also feeds for itself. It usually feeds on its mother's milk.

Genetic problems

Some babies are born with a **genetic condition**. This is a problem caused by a mistake in the **genes** (body instructions). Luckily, this is rare.

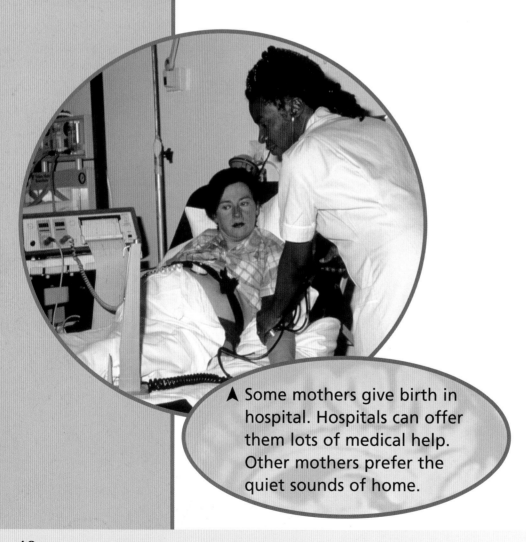

▲ Some mothers give birth in hospital. Hospitals can offer them lots of medical help. Other mothers prefer the quiet sounds of home.

Body language genetic condition medical problem caused by a mistake in the genes

The problem may be in the way its body has developed. It might have one finger too many. Or it might have a gap in the roof of its mouth. Doctors treat these problems as soon as possible.

But some genetic problems do not show up until later. They might affect the baby's heart. Or they can affect the way its brain works.

Lots of babies
Around the world, a baby is born every three seconds. Each one will be different to everyone else.

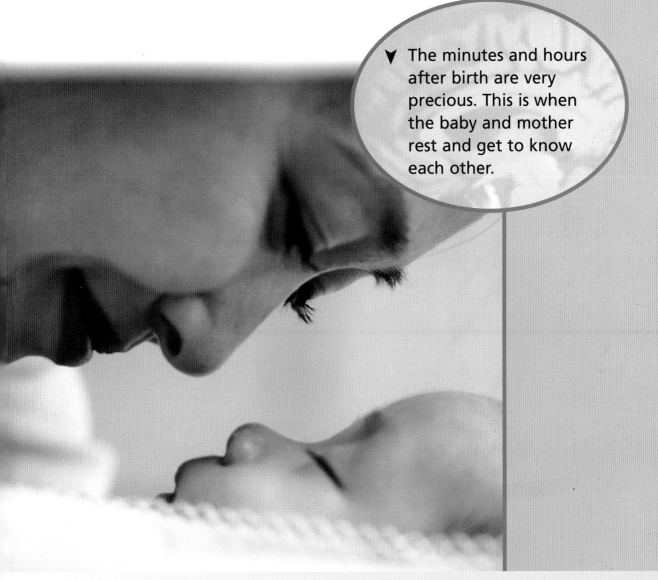

▼ The minutes and hours after birth are very precious. This is when the baby and mother rest and get to know each other.

In the genes

Genes have many effects on our lives. They decide our skin colour and hair type. They decide our height as an adult.

Changing genes

Medical scientists are trying to find ways to change some genes. This is called **gene therapy**. They are doing this to treat problems caused by mistakes in the genes. Gene therapy is a great hope for the future.

gene therapy   treating a medical condition by altering or replacing faulty genes

Taking care

Our bodies are affected by the way we take care of them. The food we eat makes a big difference. The activities we do make a big difference. The way we behave also makes a difference.

Your genes have a lot of say in what you will become. But so do the choices you make in life.

◀ Our genes have many effects on us. But so do our choices and behaviour.

Find out more

Did you know?

In each **cell** there is far more **DNA** than is needed. Some DNA does not carry the body's instructions, or **genes**. It is like blank pages in a book. These "blank pages" are called junk DNA. Scientists are not sure what they are for. But they may have useful jobs. They may control the genes.

Books

The Reproductive System, Steve Parker (Heinemann Library, 2003)

Genes and DNA, Richard Walker (Kingfisher, 2003)

Reproduction and Growth, Michaela Miller (Franklin Watts, 2005)

World Wide Web

The Internet can tell you more about your genes and reproduction. You can use a search engine or search directory.

Type in keywords such as:

- genes
- DNA
- human reproduction
- brain
- cell division
- genetic fingerprints

Search tips

There are billions of pages on the Internet. It can be difficult to find what you are looking for.

These search skills will help you find useful websites more quickly:

- Know exactly what you want to find out about.
- Use two to six keywords in a search. Put the most important words first.
- Only use names of people, places, or things.

Where to search

Search engine

A search engine looks through millions of pages. It lists all the sites that match the words in the search box. You will find the best matches are at the top of the list, on the first page. Try **bbc.co.uk/search**

Search directory

A person instead of a computer has sorted a search directory. You can search by keyword or subject and browse through the different sites. It is like looking through books on a library shelf. Try **yahooligans.com**

Glossary

cells tiny "building blocks" that make up all body parts

chromosome thread of DNA

DNA (deoxyribonucleic acid) substance that contains the body instructions, or genes

dominant when one version of a gene is stronger than another. The dominant gene's instructions are followed.

egg cell cell made by the female body

ejaculation muscle-powered action that pushes sperm out of the male body

embryo developing baby that is less than eight weeks old

fertilized egg the result of an egg cell joining with a sperm cell

fetus developing baby in the womb, from eight weeks old until birth

gene therapy treating a medical condition by altering or replacing faulty genes

genes instructions for how the body grows, develops, and works

genetic condition medical problem caused by a mistake in the genes

genetic fingerprint code on a strand of DNA. This code is different for each person.

inheritance when something gets passed from parent to child because of genes

mutation when DNA is not copied exactly

nucleus control centre of a cell

ovaries two female body parts that make egg cells

penis male body part. Sperm is released through the penis.

pregnancy time before birth when a baby develops inside the mother. In humans this lasts about nine months.

puberty when a human's reproductive parts begin to work

recessive when one version of a gene is weaker than another. The recessive gene's instructions are not always followed.

reproduction when living things make more of their kind. In humans, this is having a baby.

sperm cell cell made by the male body

stem cells cells that can make many different kinds of cells

testes two parts below the lower male body. They make sperm cells.

tumour abnormal lump or growth

unique unlike anything or anyone else

urethra tube that carries sperm out of the male body

vagina passageway from the womb to the outside of the female body

womb female body part where a baby develops. It is also called the uterus.

Index